Heart Songs

WRITTEN AND ILLUSTRATED BY
JONI FRANKS

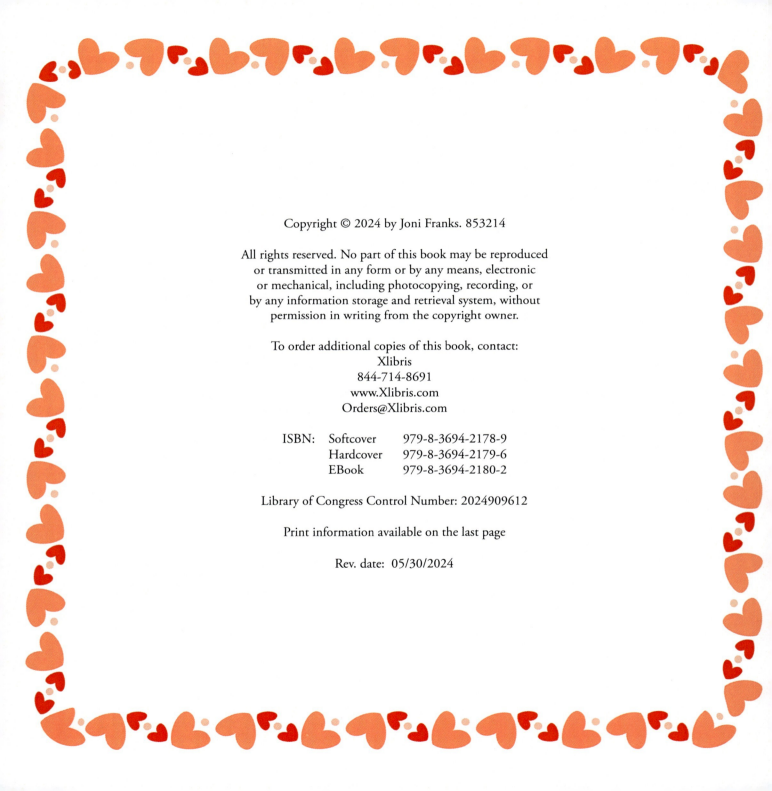

To order additional copies of this book, contact:
Xlibris
844-714-8691
www.Xlibris.com
Orders@Xlibris.com

ISBN: Softcover   979-8-3694-2178-9
       Hardcover   979-8-3694-2179-6
       EBook   979-8-3694-2180-2

Library of Congress Control Number: 2024909612

Print information available on the last page

Rev. date: 05/30/2024

Books by Joni Franks

Corky Tails: Tales of a Tailless Dog Named Sagebrush Book Series:

Corky Tails

Sagebrush Meets the Shuns

Sagebrush and the Smoke Jumper

Sagebrush and the Butterfly Creek Flood

Sagebrush and the Warm Springs Discovery

Rabos Taponados

Corky Tails Coloring Book

Sagebrush and the Disappearing Dark Sky

Sagebrush and the Never Summer Mountains

Holly Berry and Mistletoe

The Crooked Forest Book Series

The Crooked Forest, Legacy of the Holey Stone

The Crooked Forest, Cloud Crazed

The Crooked Forest, Beyond

Heart Songs

Contents

Songs of the Heart 1

Nature 11

The Love of a Dog 23

Faith 29

Songs of the Heart

When our hearts are broken

We sometimes lose our way

Yielding to emotion

And disengaging from our days

But hope can spring eternal

From our power deep within

Gifting us the strength

To aspire once again

I picked a flower in my dreams

It was beautiful to see

But when I woke, I realized

There were no blooms for me

There was a star once in my life

But that light no longer shines

Our love has passed

And slipped away

Into another time

Through the highs and the lows

Together we go

Sometimes having our say

Sometimes losing our way

Through the joy and the strife

May we remain companions for life

When I was young, I met a man

He meant everything to me

He gave me a gold band

For my left hand

And I was filled with security

In those days his green eyes blazed

Mirroring his love for me

To this day I remember those flames

Though he is gone for eternity

When we choose forgiveness

Our grief will melt away

Lessening our burdens

And brightening up our days

It is not a simple task

To heal a shattered heart

We must free the past forever

To create a fresh start

Oh, to fall in love freely

Free from the scars of the past

Minus the battles that are bound to be fought

Before the end comes at last

Oh, to be free of the heart pain

That always seems to remain

Once it's over and done with

And we try to love once again

There's hurt within this painful place

Where the crack runs through my heart

I'm searching for a new home base

New beginnings and fresh starts

Be mindful of your conduct

Don't cause your loved ones pain

Hurtful actions will not fade

Within the spirit plane

Nature

Lost in this wild place on the night of Samhain

Further away from where I have been

Colorful leaves embracing the trees

Laughing fairies call out to me

The singing hawthorn draws me in

Requesting that I enter its den

Within the dark forest

There once lived a hare

As swift as the eagle

That glides through the air

No legend no song

Or folktale compares

To the story of Kai

The magical hare

Everything is alive

Nothing truly dies

Shifting into changing forms

Wandering far and wide

Interweaving lives like vines

Creating unique storylines

Planting seeds early on

Growing roots forming bonds

Creations blowing in the breeze

Living life as they please

Before this flash in time is gone

And has slipped into the great beyond

As the moon waxes and wanes

In the course of a year

Peaking then pausing to change

Set your intentions

Birth your dreams

To see what you may gain

Queen of spring, we honor you

On this special day

As the leaves turn green

And the flowers bloom

We pay tribute to your name

It is now the time

To plant our seeds

All along our way

As we ask for fairy blessings

On this joyful Beltane day

Look up at the stars held in the sky

Sparkling stars dazzling my eyes

The stars are there even during the day

I must be clever to find a way

For the stars to guide me as they say

But how will I know which way to go

If the stars do not twinkle so?

We are dancing today

With joy in our hearts

By the end of the day

We will be ready to start

This season will shift

And there will be change

As all the earth

Will soon rearrange

There is no beginning

There is no end

Just a cycle

That begins once again

Follow the seasons

And honor your path

Keeping faith and knowing that

There is no beginning

There is no end

Just a cycle

That begins once again

The Love of a Dog

We've been together before

I know this for sure

When I look in your eyes

On that very first day

When you came to stay

Our hearts entwined as one

There's no need to say

What you silently convey

By placing your trust in me

There's a feeling of home

That I feel in my bones

When you're by my side

Our bond is so real

I instinctively feel

That you are becoming ill

As we share each day

And the years pass away

I gift you all of my love

I believe in the love of a loyal dog

I have faith in the goodness held in a woman's heart

Together they share an authentic beauty and a devoted bond

The beautiful pairing of a woman and her dog

Through thick and thin we travel

You are always by my side

Exploring and adventuring

Seeing what we may find

These mountains aren't an easy place

But we choose to stay

Waking up together

To greet every single day

Thank you, dear Sagebrush

I never want our time to end

But mostly I want to thank you

For being my best friend.

I built a special place

In the corner of my heart

Keeping faith that you'll be safe

Please stay and don't depart

In this space the music plays

And the flowers smell so sweet

It's where I want to spend my days

As long as your heart beats

When the heart stops beating

The sound of the beat remains

Leaving a bit of oneself behind

Before entering the spirit plane

When the winds of change come blowing

As they surely will

May the gusts blow soft and warm

Gently on your skin

May your soul be firmly sown

With the seeds of bravery

And may your journey be illuminated

By your own strong energy

Mother spirit, come to me

I call on you so that I can be

Confident, happy, and whole again

And find my strength that resides within

My faith in Him will never bend

He is all things known to men

He gives me all that I might need

He fills my heart

He perceives my dreams

So when I feel alone in life

No mother, no father

No husband, no wife

I rely on great courage

And walk in His path

Making mistakes but knowing that

He is always there

And I am never alone

Until the time

When He calls me home

When better days seem far away

When the light won't come

And the darkness stays

Believe in yourself

And keep hope in your heart

These times will pass

They've played their part

One cycle begins

And a different one ends

Soon we will feel

Hopeful again

We all have the power to transform the world by example

By teaching life lessons like learning to share and having respect for Mother Earth

We shall strive to be the best of who we are and who we can become

By changing the world one heart at a time

Printed in the United States
by Baker & Taylor Publisher Services